APR 2 2 2014

ELK GROVE VILLAGE PUBLIC LIBRARY
3 1250 01067 8294

W9-BNR-985

Discarded By Elk Grove
Village Public Library

ELK GROVE VILLAGE PUBLIC LIBRARY
1001 WELLINGTON AVE
ELK GROVE VILLAGE, IL 60007
(847) 439-0447

City Safari

Pigeon

Isabel Thomas

Heinemann
LIBRARY

Chicago, Illinois

© 2014 Heinemann Library
an imprint of Capstone Global Library, LLC
Chicago, Illinois

To contact Capstone Global Library please phone 800-747-4992, or visit our web site www.capstonepub.com

All rights reserved. No part of this publication may be reproduced or transmitted in any form or by any means, electronic or mechanical, including photocopying, recording, taping, or any information storage and retrieval system, without permission in writing from the publisher.

Edited by Dan Nunn, Rebecca Rissman, and Helen Cox Cannons
Designed by Tim Bond
Original illustrations © Capstone Global Library Ltd 2014
Picture research by Mica Brancic
Production by Helen McCreath
Originated by Capstone Global Library Ltd
Printed and bound in China

17 16 15 14 13
10 9 8 7 6 5 4 3 2 1

Library of Congress Cataloging-in-Publication Data
Thomas, Isabel, 1980-
  Pigeon / Isabel Thomas.
    pages cm.—(City safari)
  Includes bibliographical references and index.
  ISBN 978-1-4329-8806-7 (hb)—ISBN 978-1-4329-8813-5 (pb)
  1. Pigeons—Juvenile literature. I. Title.

QL696.C63T49 2014
598.6'5—dc23   2013017274

Acknowledgments
The author and publisher are grateful to the following for permission to reproduce copyright material: Alamy pp. 16 & 23 pest (both © Caro/Muhs); FLPA p. 8 (Imagebroker); Getty Images p. 11 (© 2009 François Angers); Naturepl.com pp. 6 (Hermansen/© Wild Wonders of Europe), 18 & 19 (both © Laurent Geslin); Shutterstock pp. 4 (© AKV), 5 (© yykkaa), 7 (© george green), 9 (© pirita), 10 (© Nikita Starichenko), 12 (© AG-Photo), 13 (© Andrzej Tokarski), 14 (© Elena Dijour), 15 (© MNStudio), 20 (© Fotofermer), 21 (© Ian Grainger), 23 mate (© Dereje), 23 breed (© Fotofermer), 23 roost (© Nikita Starichenko), 23 sense (© OPIS Zagreb), 23 flock (© yykkaa); SuperStock p. 17 (Design Pics/Artzooks).

Front cover photograph of a pigeon reproduced with permission of Shutterstock (© DanVostok). Back cover photograph of a pigeon drinking water reproduced with permission of Shutterstock (© Andrzej Tokarski).

We would like to thank Michael Bright for his invaluable help in the preparation of this book.

Every effort has been made to contact copyright holders of any material reproduced in this book. Any omissions will be rectified in subsequent printings if notice is given to the publisher.

Warning!

Never touch wild animals or their homes. Some wild animals carry diseases. Never go near a pigeon's nest. Pigeons may peck or scratch to protect their babies.

Note About Spotter Icon

Your eyes, ears, and nose can tell you if a pigeon is nearby. Look for these clues as you read the book, and find out more on page 22.

Contents

Some words are shown in bold, **like this**.
You can find them in the glossary on page 23.

Who Has Been Caught Stealing Some Food?

black wing-bars

white bump

red feet

Blue-gray feathers. Short legs. Red feet. It's a pigeon!

You don't have to visit the country to see wildlife.

1

shiny green and purple feathers

Towns and cities are home to wild animals, too.

Come on a city safari. Find out if pigeons are living near you.

Why Do Pigeons Live in Towns and Cities?

In the country, birds like pigeons live near cliffs and mountains.

These are safe places to build nests.

Pigeons can find everything they need in towns and cities, too.

There are warm, high places to find shelter, and there is plenty of food to eat.

What Makes Pigeons Good at Living in Towns and Cities?

Pigeons are not scared of bright lights and loud noises.

They do not mind being close to people.

Pigeons can see, smell, and hear very well.

They can **sense** danger, and fly away quickly.

Where Do Pigeons Rest?

Pigeons are most active in the morning. They rest and sunbathe in the afternoon.

Large **flocks** gather in high places that are sheltered from the wind.

Buildings and bridges are safe places for pigeons to **roost** at night.

Pigeons also sleep inside of roofs and empty buildings.

What Do Pigeons Eat and Drink?

Pigeons like to eat seeds and grain.

They may fly outside of towns and cities to peck at farmers' fields.

Backyards and parks are good places to find a drink.

Pigeons use their beaks like straws to suck up water.

Why Do Pigeons Like Living Near People?

Some pigeons might never leave their town or city.

Parks, backyards, and streets are full of food that people have thrown away.

In some towns and cities, people feed pigeons birdseed.

Pigeons are smart. They learn who will feed them and who will chase them away.

What Dangers Do Pigeons Face?

Many pigeons are trapped and killed because they are **pests**.

Pigeon droppings are messy, and can damage buildings and machines.

Pigeons' nests and feathers can block gutters and drainpipes.

People worry that pigeons spread disease if they go near cafés or restaurants.

Where Do Pigeons Lay Eggs?

Many city pigeons can **breed** at any time of the year.

When they are ready to **mate**, males puff out their neck feathers and do a dance.

The female pigeon lays two eggs in the nest.

Both pigeons take turns to keep the eggs warm until they hatch.

How Can I Spot a Baby Pigeon?

pink bump

large beak

Baby pigeons stay in the nest until they are one or two months old.

When they leave, they are almost fully grown.

Young pigeons look slightly different from adults.

Their beaks look big, and the bump at the top is pink rather than white.

Pigeon Spotter's Guide

Look back at the sights, sounds, and smells that tell you a pigeon might be nearby. Use these clues to go on your own city safari.

1. Look for pigeons of different colors. City pigeons can be pale brown, white, or patterned.

2. Pigeons make soft bubbling and cooing sounds.

3. Droppings help you spot places where pigeons have been.

4. While the female gets ready to lay her eggs, the male collects twigs, leaves, and other things to build up the nest. Pigeons build their nests in sheltered places.

Picture Glossary

 **breed** when a male and female animal mate and have babies

 **flock** group of birds eating, resting, or flying together

 **mate** when a male and female animal get together to have babies

 **pest** animal that causes damage to people's belongings and homes, or other buildings

 **roost** settle down to rest or sleep

 **sense** find out what is around through sight, hearing, smell, taste, and touch

Find Out More

Books

Piehl, Janet. *Let's Look at Pigeons.* Minneapolis, Minn.: Lerner, 2010.

Roza, Greg. *Your Neighbor the Pigeon.* New York: Windmill, 2012.

Web sites

FactHound offers a safe, fun way to find Internet sites related to this book. All of the sites on FactHound have been researched by our staff.

Here's all you do:
Visit www.facthound.com
Type in this code: 9781432988067

Index